Keeping Your Baby Safe!

KEEPING YOUR BABY SAFE

"I thoroughly enjoyed reading *Keeping Your Baby Safe.* As a first time mother, I found many of the safety tips helpful. The checklists were especially handy. Prevention is the key to keeping children safe, and I believe that this book is an up-to-date guide on creating a safe environment. As a teacher, I found this book to be well written and very informative."

> – Carla Perakes, B.S., M.A.
> Adjunct Assistant Professor
> Middle Tennessee State University
> Murfreesboro, Tennessee

"I feel this is a book that new parents will find especially helpful as a ready reference in child safety. This book is easy to read and has some good checklists for parents to consider when trying to childproof areas inside and outside their home."

> – Jane Y. Scott, M.D.
> Neonatologist
> St. Joseph Hospital
> Denver, Colorado

"This is an outstanding book to assist parents in keeping their children safe in the home. Checklists capture the essential safety principles. These guide the parents, step-by-step, in making changes in their environment. A "MUST" for all parents."

> – Eleanor Paquette, R.N., B.S.N., P.H.N.
> Education Consultant
> Author: "Patient Education Standards"
> 5th edition

"June Dyche has the unique ability to be both comprehensive and simple. This book offers the best road map I have seen for preventing childhood accidents. It is the most complete, readable and useful book on child safety."

> – Ginny Dudek, R.N., B.S.N., M.Ed.
> Clinical Research Nurse Coordinator
> Department Pediatrics
> University of North Carolina
> at Chapel Hill

Acknowledgments

- - - Christine Barkoukis Hoey, R.N., B.S.N., for manuscript review
- - - Romayne Pratt, B.A., for layout design
- - - Norm for his encouragement and support
- - - Jane Scott, M.D., for manuscript review and helpful suggestions.

Manufactured in the United States of America

First Edition

The suggestions, procedures and other materials in this book are not intended as a substitute for consultation with your physician or health care provider.

The contents of this book have been reviewed by medical professionals. The publisher disclaims all responsibility arising from any adverse effects or results that may occur as a result of the inappropriate application of any information in this book.

© 1994 TriOak Education
3698 Armstrong Valley Road
Murfreesboro, TN 37129

ISBN # 0-9609732-4-9

TABLE OF CONTENTS

Introduction

Your child is the most precious thing in the world to you! From infancy and throughout childhood, you must be observant in protecting your child from accidents and potential danger.

This guidebook is dedicated to helping you prevent your child from accidents and harm.

As an infant, your baby is helpless. With growth and development, a drive to touch, taste and discover becomes prominent. As the world expands, the risks multiply. You can help make your baby's environment safe.

This guide will highlight potential hazards. The tips and reminders may help you protect your child from painful experiences, unnecessary tears and possible life-threatening dangers.

Part One

KEEPING YOUR BABY SAFE

2- Keeping Your Baby Safe

Accidents

Accidents are unexpected events which can hurt people and damage things. They are caused by unsafe conditions and unsafe people. By following the guidelines in the book, you can prevent an accident.

Safety

Safety means being free from risk or danger. Remove dangerous conditions . . . be safe.

Unsafe Conditions

Dangerous conditions may be present in the home environment. Look around you. It is important to notice them. It is better to take action to eliminate the unsafe situations.

Unsafe People

It is important to have knowledge, skills and good judgment before taking action. Observe your surroundings. Plan Ahead. Think about what you are going to do; know your limits. Be especially careful if you are tired or upset. This is the time when accidents have a tendency to occur.

Accidents Don't Have to Happen to You

The problem with accidents is that they are unexpected. In the middle of an accident you don't have time to do much, except . . . get hurt.

The KEY to managing accidents is to PREVENT them. Spend a few minutes reviewing your surroundings. Eliminating a hazard can save days or years of pain and suffering.

You Can Prevent Accidents

Accidents don't just happen; something makes them happen. Take some precautions. The information on the following pages will outline many. Give yourself a pat on the back for the ways you are already acting safely.

SAFETY NOTE

A household utility which contributes to many child accidents is the telephone. Many tragedies occur while a caregiver leaves the child unattended . . . "just for a minute." It may be helpful to buy a cordless telephone to keep yourself mobile so you can talk on the phone and observe your child.

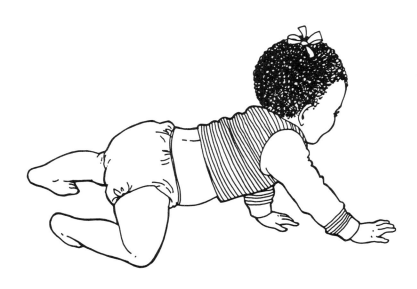

GENERAL SAFETY GUIDELINES

NEVER smoke, drink or carry hot items while carrying your baby.

NEVER tie pacifiers, jewelry or anything around your child's neck.

NEVER use a throw rug or area rug at the top of a stairway. Buy throw rugs that have slip resistant backing if you use them anywhere.

NEVER place humidifiers, heaters, fans or other electrical appliances within reach of your child.

NEVER put pails or pans of water on the floor near your child. A child who falls head first into a pail of water may not have the strength to get out.

NEVER put children's toys in high traffic areas or on stairs. Family members may trip over them.

NEVER allow buttons, pins, coins, paper clips or other small items to remain on the carpets or floors. These are potential danger items for swallowing or choking.

Note: Anything your child can reach which is small is likely to end up in the mouth.

NEVER leave your child with a babysitter under twelve years of age or in an environment where there are too many children and few caretakers. Review with your babysitters how to respond quickly in an emergency.

NEVER leave an infant or small child alone even for an instant in a tub or near a pool, ditch or pond. Do not take a child onto a boat or flotation device without the child wearing a life vest.

NEVER leave plastic grocery bags out where a child can reach and play with them. Request paper bags which are safe and can be recycled.

NEVER bicycle with a child unless you are a good rider. Have the child wear a helmet and secure him or her in a passenger seat. If you are riding with your child, keep your bike behind the youngster.

NEVER allow your toddler or preschooler to play in the street or near parked cars.

NEVER leave your child at home alone . . . not even for a few minutes. Don't ever take this chance!

NEVER give your children under the age of four years ice, grapes, nuts, popcorn, pitted fruits, hard candy or other food items which may lead to choking.

NEVER leave a loaded firearm in the house if children will ever be present. Many tragedies occur by accidental discharging of a loaded gun. If you own a gun, unload it and store the ammunition separately from the gun. Keep the gun locked in a gun case.

NEVER put a child in hot water without testing the temperature of the water. Many burn accidents occur each year to infants and children. Set the thermostat on your hot water heater under 120°F. Test the temperature of your own hot water by letting it run a few minutes from the faucet that is closest to your hot water heater. Use a meat or candy thermometer to measure the temperature. If it is above 120°F., turn the thermostat on your hot water down to a lower setting. Wait a day for the water to reach the temperature . . . test again.

YOUR HOUSE . . . A Safer Place

While there is no substitute for your close observation, there are things you can do to make your house a safer place. If you do these carefully and well in advance, you can eliminate dangers and make life pleasant for the entire family.

Door Safety
Interior Doors

Check all interior doors to make certain that none can be locked from the inside without access from the outside. Find all keys for doors which have locks. Remove locks for which you have no keys.

Doors with "push-button" locks should have a small hole on the outside knob. A coat hanger piece or large hairpin inserted into the hole will unlock the door. Keep the key or unlocking device handy and out of reach by hanging it high on a nail outside the door.

At times a towel thrown over the top of a door will prevent it from closing tightly. Be certain that the child cannot pull the towel off.

Exterior Doors

Exterior doors should be kept closed, locked or latched at all times. Install extra latches high out of the child's reach. ANY door which leads to a stairway, garage or other unsafe area should have extra latches.

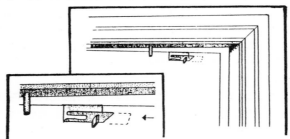

Safety Door Latch

A doorknob cover fits over an existing doorknob. When gripped by an adult or older child tightly, the doorknob will turn. It is difficult for a young child to turn this covered knob.

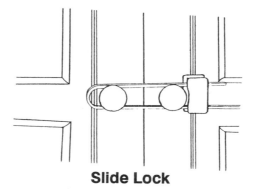

Slide Lock

These devices may be purchased from your Hardware Store. These have been specifically designed for child safety and easy installation.

Electrical Safety

Electrical Safety is an important process to deal with as it relates to Childproofing Your Home. A 110-volt shock is not only frightening . . . it is dangerous.

* Cover all electrical outlets with plastic safety caps.

* Unplug appliances such as hair dryers and curling irons when not in use.

* Keep electrical cords away from toddlers who might chew on them. This accident could burn off part of the lip or end of the tongue.

* Teach your child not to turn on lights or electrical appliances while standing on a wet floor or wet ground.

* Teach your child NEVER to touch an electrical appliance while the child is in the bathtub. This can result in immediate electrocution if the appliance is plugged in . . . even if the switch is turned to "off."

* Never leave light bulb sockets empty when lamps are plugged in.

* Keep electrical fans and heaters out of your child's reach.

Electric Cords

The most common injuries caused by electric cords are burns to the mouth and face when the child chews on a cord.

*   Lamp cords and small appliance cords should not dangle from a table. Secure cords so that a child cannot tug the cord and pull down the appliance. Move the table against the wall; wedge the cord between the wall and table.

*   Avoid use of extension cords. If used, wrap the electrical tape around the connection so that the appliance plug cannot be pulled out of the extension cord.

Cord Caution

According to the Consumer Product Safety Commission, 119 children strangled on the loop ends of cords from venetian blinds and draperies between 1981 and 1991. Most of the victims were younger than two. If available in your area, purchase Venetian blinds with break-apart cords.

Plastic Cord Shortener

Use a plastic cord shortener or electrical tape to wind up excess cord. Tuck it out of reach. Extra cord length can lead to strangulation.

Plastic Cord Shortener

Cover all electrical outlets with a device or change outlets to twist style. Burns or electric shock may occur when little fingers insert something into an outlet. Paper clips, pins, etc. may be found and inserted into uncovered, unprotected outlets.

Styles of Outlet Covers

Snap On

This style is most difficult for children to open. Relies on Strength.

Twist Style

Automatically twists closed when plug is removed. Insert plug prongs into safety plate. Turn plug clockwise and push it into outlet.

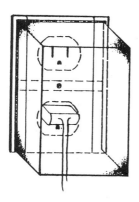

Snap On

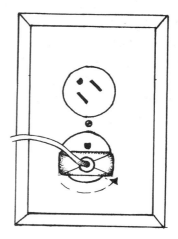

Twist Style

Permanent

Permanent outlet cover must be opened and closed with a screwdriver. Blank plates can be used for outlets you want to keep permanently closed.

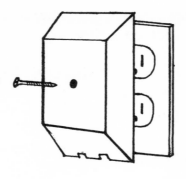
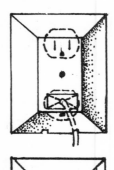

Outlet Cap

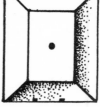

Outlet caps are plastic two-pronged disks that fit into an existing outlet. When purchasing, test them to make certain they are tight fitting. Check for Underwriter's Laboratory (UL) approval. When caps are removed, they may be misplaced and leave the outlet exposed. The caps are also small enough to become a choking hazard. To remove this problem, select the type that attaches to the outlet plate screw with a tether strap. Refer to illustration.

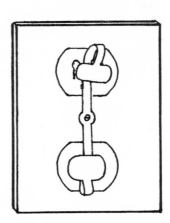

Outlet Cap

Glass Doors

Sliding glass doors need special attention. Apply decals on the glass at your child's eye level. This will focus attention that caution is necessary.

Check to be certain that the glass is a safety glass. This should be listed on one corner of the door.

If there is a screen with the glass door, in warmer weather lock the screen door.

A locking bar works for sliding doors and windows. When the bar is in a "down" or "lock" position, it wedges the sliding door or window shut. When the bar is in a raised position, the sliding door or window can be moved.

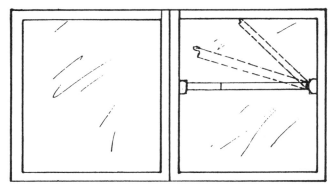

Locking Bar

Window Safety

Check the windows in your home carefully. Your child should not have access to the outside through a window. Check all screens to ensure that they are secure and free of torn spots. A child should not be able to push a screen up or out. Every window should have a latch that is high and out of a child's reach. Equip windows with guards or safety latches. They come in a variety of sizes and styles. Most hardware stores carry a variety for all types of windows. Window guards are installed inside the frame to prevent entry or exit. The window may still be opened.

Window guards or latches cannot be removed quickly. They should not be used on windows which may be needed as a fire escape.

* If you have double-hung windows that can open from the top, it is better to open the windows from the top.

* Remove crank handles from windows. A child may be tempted to open the window using the handle.

* Check blinds to be sure that edges are not sharp. Window blind cords and drapery cords should be wound and placed out of reach.

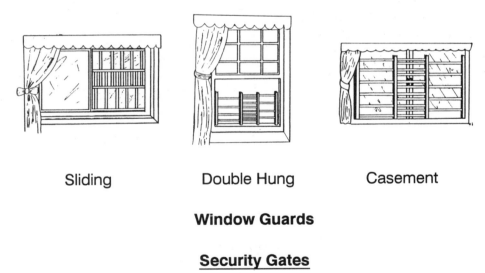

| Sliding | Double Hung | Casement |

Window Guards

Security Gates

Security gates come in a variety of styles and sizes. Install them in doors leading to stairs or rooms which contain items which might be dangerous to your child. The Consumer Product Safety Commission warns against expandable gates with V shaped or diamond shaped openings along the edge. These edges may pinch or trap children. Select a gate with a straight top edge. The gate should have rigid mesh, plastic screen or narrowly spaced metal or wooden slats.

Install according to the manufacturer's directions. Check pressure-bar gates to make sure they are strong enough to resist the pressure exerted by a child. If you use a pressure-bar gate, install it with the pressure bar away from the child. (The pressure bar is often used by a child for climbing.)

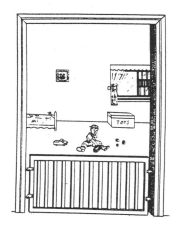

Security Gate

Always latch the security gate securely. A child may lean against the gate. If it is not latched well . . . an accident may occur.

Furniture

Look at your furniture from a safety basis and through the eyes of your child.

* Remove any free standing screens or partitions. These may become falling and pinching hazards.

* Check the furniture to be certain that no pieces are in danger of toppling over.

* In place of floor or table lamps which a child can easily tip over, use a wall or ceiling lamp.

* Keep a television set on a low, solidly-placed piece of furniture instead of a weak TV stand or cart.

* Look for pieces of furniture that are freely movable or fold. Chairs on casters, rocking chairs, deck chairs and drop-leaf tables may pinch or become potential safety hazards.

* Sharp edges of furniture can cause cuts, bumps or bruises. Corners can be made safer by taping foam or fabric to the corner and edge. Edge and corner cushions which are made specifically for this purpose can be purchased.

* Look for loose nails, screws or bolts and remove them. If unable to do so, you may need to remove the specific furniture piece temporarily.

* Look for tacks or staples in upholstered furniture. Be certain that the fabric is intact and no padding can surface. Check for buttons, loose piping and for presence of loose coins, pencils and items which may have dropped in the cushions.

* Check all furniture pieces for drawers or cabinets. Place safety latches on all drawers to prevent them from being pulled out. Cabinets may also need to have locks placed on them.

* If you have glass table tops, remove items which may break the glass. Glass top tables are not recommended.

* Bookshelves need special attention. Clear all lower shelves of figurines, glass objects, lighters or dried or live flower arrangements.

* On lower shelves, squeeze the books tightly so they remain firm and steady. If the shelves reach to the floor and can be used as a ladder, move another piece of furniture in front to prevent the child from climbing higher.

Stairs and Hallways

Your child will consider climbing stairs as an exciting experience. Work closely with the child to make this a safe and fun time. Climbing up stairs may come more easily and naturally. The safest way down, in the beginning, is for the child to crawl down backward on hands and knees. Later in the learning experience, the handrail becomes a safety device for the child to use.

> Until your child has mastered the stairs, keep the security gates in place.

* Stair and hallway areas must be kept well lit at all times.

* Check stairs for loose risers, loose carpeting and loose carpet tacks.

* Keep hallways and stairs free of loose rugs, toys, clothing or items which may cause tripping.

* Be certain stairways have handrails. Check to see that they are secure.

Household Plants

House plants add a great deal of enjoyment to the family in any home. Adding flowers and greenery to the house brings in part of the outdoor feeling that makes us feel comfortable in our surroundings. It is important to note that many common house and garden plants can harm a child. Portions of a plant and in some cases, an entire plant, can be toxic and has the potential of being extremely dangerous. The following lists outline household plants that are safe (non-harmful) and others that are poisonous. The outdoor yard plants are listed in Section Four, page 56. Some plants are listed in both the indoor and outdoor section. Often the plant is grown outdoors, and part may be brought indoors as a decorative arrangement; for example, azaleas, roses and tulips.

Make a tour of your home and list the plants that you have. Many have identification labels. (It is good to keep these on the plant for future reference.) As you identify them, refer to the following lists to see if they are harmful. If you find that some are, remove them from your home immediately. Remember, children love to climb. All plants, even hanging plants, can become a target for your child's attention. Don't take chances. If you have a plant that is not listed here, remove it so that your child is unable to get to it. Call your Poison Control Center for information.

Poisonous Common House Plants

Azalea*   Iris
Caladium (fancy leaf caladium) Monstera (swiss cheese plant)
Colocasia (elephant's ear)   Narcissus (narcissus,
Delphinium (larkspur)   daffodil, jonquil)
Dieffenbachia (dumb cane)   Philodendron
                                                   (elephant ear)
    * Grown outdoors - brought in as decorative flower

Non-Harmful Common House Plants

African Violet   Carnation   Monkey Plant
Aralia   Christmas Cactus   Piggyback Plant
Asparagus Fern   Chrysanthemum   Rubber Plant
Aster   Coleus   Snapdragon
Baby's Breath   Creeping Charlie   Spider Plant
Bachelor Buttons   Daisies   Swedish Ivy
Begonia   Ferns (most types) Tulip
Boston Fern   Gardenia   Violet
Bromeliads   Mint   Wandering Jew

This list is meant as a general guide. Consult your doctor or Poison Control Center for more information.

18- Keeping Your Baby Safe

A SAFETY WALK

ITEM	☺ YES	☹ NO
Are glass doors marked with decals at your child's eye level?	☐	☐
Are windows properly locked and screens secure?	☐	☐
Do you keep sliding doors closed? When open, are screens locked?	☐	☐
Are firearms out of sight, unloaded, and locked?	☐	☐
Are unused electrical outlets covered with dummy plugs?	☐	☐
Do you check and reposition dangling cords, strings, lamp cords, clotheslines?	☐	☐
Are the edges of the furniture covered with rubber protectors?	☐	☐
Do you keep plastic grocery bags out of reach?	☐	☐
Are area rugs slip resistant?	☐	☐

ITEM	☺ YES	☹ NO
Are your floors and surrounding area free of items which can cause choking such as balloons, plastic bags, small toys, Legos,® plastic wrap, buttons, pins?	☐	☐
Did you push dangerous or breakable items toward the center of the table?	☐	☐
Do you check electrical cords to make sure they are not frayed?	☐	☐
Are the stairs well lit and equipped with handrails?	☐	☐
Do you have a safety gate?	☐	☐
Have you checked the temperature of the water in your hot water heater?	☐	☐
Are your exterior doors locked when not in use?	☐	☐

A Nice and Safe Visit

Part Two

CHILDPROOFING YOUR HOME

CHILDPROOFING YOUR HOME

What You Need to Know

Did you know that every month nearly 400 children under four years of age die in the United States because of accidents? Most of these accidents can be prevented. Often, accidents happen because parents are not aware of what the child can do. Your child is a fast learner. He or she will suddenly be able to roll over, crawl, sit and stand. The child may climb before walking, or walk with support months before you expect it.   A common accident is a baby rolling off a changing table or a bed.

Many parents find it easier to "babyproof" or "childproof" their homes than to watch their baby's every move.

Get down on your hands and knees -- crawl from room to room looking at things from your baby's viewpoint and for things within a toddlers' reach. If you have other children, let them join you.

Kitchen

Most kitchens are the "hub" of family activity. The family may spend more waking hours here than in any other room. There are many "potential" dangers which can be eliminated.

Dishwashers, ovens, and microwaves can be secured with appliance latches. They attach easily with adhesive backs to the sides of tops of appliances.

The dishwasher holds items such as knives and glassware your child should not reach.

* Keep dishwasher's closing latch in locked position.

* Put soap in dishwasher when you are ready to run it -- <u>not</u> before.

* Place knives and sharp utensils with sharp edges pointing down.

* Remove stove knobs or install stove knob covers.

* Never use cupboards over stove to store cookies, candies, or other things your child may want to reach.

* Locate microwave where child cannot reach controls.

Refrigerator magnets should be put away.

* Magnets can become loose and drop to the floor. They may end up in the child's mouth.

Small appliances such as toasters, coffee makers, and food processors need to be at the back of the counter.

* Check that cords are not dangling over the edge of the counter.

* Unplug the cords when the appliances are not in use.

* Never use electric woks, deep fryers or frying pans near your child. Keep cords and handles out of reach. Spilled oils cause severe burns.

* Install safety covers over the electrical outlets.

Cabinets and drawers may contain harmful items.

* Use cabinet latches. They are inexpensive and easy to install.

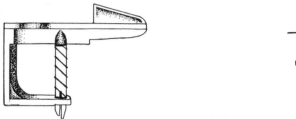 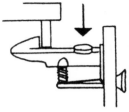

Drawer Latch

Any products that could be harmful need to be locked up, even things like dried beans.

LOCK UP THESE KITCHEN ITEMS

» Cooking utensils	» Knives
» Silverware/cutlery	» Glassware
» Scissors	» Vegetable peeler
» Breakable dishes	» Pet food
» Trash bags	» Plastic bags
» Plastic wrap	» Foil
» Rubber bands	» Batteries
» Can opener	» Nutcracker and pick
» Graters/slicers	» Pencils
» Coins	» Buttons
» Soap and dishwasher detergent	

Note: You may want to allow your child access to one cabinet containing old pots and pans. Babies and toddlers enjoy playing and listening to the sounds they make.

KITCHEN CHECKLIST

ITEM	☺ YES	☹ NO
Are knives out of reach?	☐	☐
Are small appliances unplugged?	☐	☐
Do you have safety latches on cabinets and appliance doors?	☐	☐
Are appliance cords not dangling over counter tops?	☐	☐
Do you avoid using slippery rugs on a tile floor?	☐	☐
Are drinking containers used by the child made of plastic?	☐	☐
Do you routinely cook on back burners and keep pot handles turned toward the back of the stove?	☐	☐

Nursery or Bedroom

Use nursery furniture and equipment safely and teach other members of the family and babysitters to do the same.

* Check your child frequently while he or she is in crib or playpen.

* Place fabric padded bumpers in the crib to protect baby's head.

* Once baby can sit up on his/her own, remove any crib gyms or mobiles.

* Once baby can pull himself or herself up to stand, set crib mattress to the lowest position.

* Check blankets, bed sheets and their edges for rips and strings.

* Do not use plastic mattress covers or pillow covers or electric blankets in crib.

* Never use a strap or harness device on your child while he or she is in the crib.

* Mobiles should be located where they cannot be reached by baby.

* Keep crib away from drapes, drapery cords, dresser tops, humidifiers, heaters, fans, lamps, and electrical outlets.

* Do not leave anything hanging over side of crib; i.e., clothing, diapers, sheets, blankets, etc. These may easily be pulled down by your child.

* If your child is under 4 months old, do not leave objects, i.e., stuffed animals, extra pillows, large toys, extra blankets, in the crib. These can smother a child.

Do not place furniture or toys under a window. A toddler may choose to crawl up to it.

Place the crib so that the sun cannot shine directly on your child.

* Check the condition of all windows to be certain glass is not cracked or broken.

* Use window latches, which prevent the window from being open more than a few inches.

* If possible, open the windows at the top of the window frame.

Place smoke alarms or heat detectors in the halls near the bedrooms. As extra protection, place one in the child's bedroom.

NURSERY OR BEDROOM CHECKLIST

ITEM	☺ YES	☹ NO
Is your baby's sleeping environment safe?	☐	☐
Is crib placed away from windows, dangling cords, blinds or draperies?	☐	☐
Is crib away from any furniture that a child may use to climb out of the crib?	☐	☐
Is baby kept away from any sinking surface such as a beanbag or similar surface which could lead to suffocation?	☐	☐

Bathroom

The only time your child should be in the bathroom is with another adult. NEVER leave a child alone (even for a few seconds). Secure bathroom door with a safety door latch. Remove dangerous items from bathroom or place items securely beyond child's reach.

* Use rubber bath mat to protect your child from slips and falls.

* If tub has glass doors, check to make certain they are made of safety glass. Install safety latches on doors.

* Turn off all hot water handles tightly so your child cannot turn them easily.

* You may want to cover faucet with a protector, so your child cannot be scraped by it.

* Use paper cups at bathroom sink, because plastic can splinter and glass can break.

* Hang hand washed items above the tub to drip-dry. A wet bathroom floor is very slippery.

* Be careful what you put in waste baskets - razor blades, empty aerosol cans and empty cleaner containers should be discarded where your child cannot reach them.

* All rugs in the bathroom should have non-skid rubber backs.

* Choose rugs that are not thick or easy to trip on.

* Install safety covers on all electrical outlets.

* Install toilet locks on all toilets. Keep toilet lid closed (could be a drowning hazard).

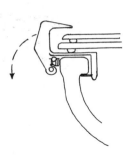

* Do not use continuous cleaning toilet bowl cleaners. Many have bleach in them.

Toilet Lock

LOCK UP THESE BATHROOM ITEMS

» Razors and razor blades

» Shaving cream

» Cosmetics

» Bath salts and bath oils

» All medicines

» Hair shampoo, conditioner, rinse

» Toilet bowl cleaner

» Scouring powder

» Bathroom cleaners

» Aerosol cans

» Antiseptics

» Vitamins

» Deodorizers and air fresheners

» Mouthwash

» Nail polish, polish remover

» Hair sprays

» Ointments

» Drain cleaner

30- Childproofing Your Home

CHECKLIST

ITEM	☺ YES	☹ NO
Do you have non-skid mats on the bottom of the tub and shower?	☐	☐
Are the faucets padded?	☐	☐
Are electrical appliances away from water?	☐	☐
Are toiletries and cosmetics out of baby's reach?	☐	☐
Do bathroom rugs have slip proof backing?	☐	☐
Is your bathroom door kept closed? Do you have a safety lock?	☐	☐
Is toilet seat down and latched?	☐	☐
Do you have plastic soap dishes (not glass)?	☐	☐
Do you drain water from the tub as soon as you are finished using it?	☐	☐

Medicine Cabinet

There are specially designed medicine cabinet latches for both hinged and sliding doors.

* It is better to remove all dangerous products from the cabinet in the bathroom (under the sink) to a high shelf in a locked closet or to a locked medicine cabinet.

* Remember prescription as well as non-prescription medicines may be poisonous for your baby.

MEDICINE CABINET CHECKLIST

ITEM	☺ YES	☹ NO
Is the cabinet latched?	☐	☐
Do you keep safety caps on medicine containers?	☐	☐
Do you keep medicines out of reach?	☐	☐
Do you dispose of "out of date" medications?	☐	☐
Are razor blades, pins, scissors out of reach?	☐	☐

Medicine Cabinet Latches

Laundry Room and Sewing Room

These rooms should be "off limits" to your child.

Use items outlined in previous section to secure doors, cabinets and cupboards.

* Never leave water standing in laundry tubs. Empty after each use.

* Place all laundry soaps, starch, stain removers, bleaches and sprays on a high shelf or lock in a cupboard or cabinet.

* Do not leave empty aerosol containers, cans or receptacles in wastebaskets. Place these items in the outdoor trash.

* Make sure your clothesline and clothespins are out of your child's reach. Cut off any excess.

* Lock your sewing machine away in a closet or cupboard. If it has its own cabinet, lock it. Unplug the sewing machine after each use.

* Keep scissors, needles, thread, buttons and sharp sewing items in a locked or latched cabinet or drawer.

* Iron when your child is napping. If the child is playing in a playpen, be certain the iron, cord or board can't be reached. Between uses, store the iron and ironing board away.

HARMFUL HOUSEHOLD SUBSTANCES/PRODUCTS

» Alcohol
» Air Freshener
» Ammonia
» Arts and Craft Supplies
» Bleaches
» Cleaners and Cleansers
» Cosmetics (nail polish, corn remover, cologne, talcum powder, permanent wave solution)
» Deodorants
» Detergents
» Disinfectants
» Fabric Softener
» Fertilizers/Plant Food

» Hair Spray
» Lye
» Medications (aspirin, iron pills, cold medicines, tranquilizers, laxatives, birth control pills)
» Mouthwash
» Paint and Paint Remover
» Pesticides
» Petroleum Products (kerosene, gasoline, furniture polish)
» Shaving Cream
» Toothpicks
» Turpentine
» Vinegar
» Weed Killers

Most Common Accidents

According to Age

Birth to Six Months (Rolling and Reaching)

* Falls off changing tables or out of infant seats
* Burns
* Crib accidents
* Auto accidents
* Choking . . . small items go directly into mouth

Six to Twelve Months (Crawling and Walking)

* High chair accidents
* Grabbing accidents . . . burns from hot drinks, cuts from glass
* Falls and cuts against sharp table corners
* Toy accidents . . . sharp edges, chewable parts, sharp toy edges
* Walker and stroller accidents
* Choking . . . trying to eat peanuts, popcorn and hot dogs
* Auto accidents

One to Two Years (Walking and Exploring)

* Ingestion of poison: most common age for poison ingestion
* Cuts
* Climbing accidents
* Exploring accidents . . . medicine cabinets, cupboards
* Unguarded water hazards . . . pools, streams, ponds
* Auto accidents
* Choking on peanuts and popcorn still possible
* Firearm accidents

Part Three

BABY EQUIPMENT

Have Fun
Keep
Safety in Mind

BABY EQUIPMENT

It is important to recognize that a baby grows and develops quickly. Equipment which you purchase must be right for today and for tomorrow when you will be concentrating on safety as well as value, attractiveness and durability. Make certain that the product you buy has complete instructions. The product should be right for the child's age, size and development. If the item requires assembly, follow the manufacturer's directions.

> Use each product with maximum safety in mind. Develop a "safety mind-set."

Playpen Safety

Play pens do have their place. Putting a child in a playpen while you answer the phone is a safety saver . . . but keep the conversation short.
A child in a playpen when you work is helpful but give the child attention frequently.

General Information for both wooden and mesh playpens

* Check that all screws and bolts are in place and that none are missing.

* Cover any exposed nuts and bolts.

* All glued joints must be secure.

* The legs and frame must be sturdy and stable.

* If staples are used: all should be firmly in place with none missing.

* Avoid dangling strings from the playpen sides.

* Remove large toys, blocks or boxes. These may be used as steps for climbing out.

Mesh Playpen

Check that the netting is small enough that it cannot catch the buttons on a child's clothing. Check that the mesh is attached to the top rail and floor plate securely. Avoid mesh with large openings. These may be used as toeholds for climbing.

Never leave your child in a mesh playpen with a side down. A baby can become trapped and can strangle in a pocket of mesh.

Wooden Playpen

Check that the bars are not so widely spaced that the baby's head can get stuck. Check to see that the slats are no more than 2-3/8" apart. Many older playpens do not conform. Be sure to measure! Check to be certain that the slats are strong and secure without splinters. Many old style wooden playpens do not have a built-in floor. This is a potential safety risk when the child becomes strong enough to push the playpen around the room.

Crib

Crib accidents are high on the list of injuries to infants. If you plan to buy a crib for a newborn, there are some safety features that are important. New cribs are required by law to have these safety features. If you are buying a used crib or borrowing one, look for these features:

■ Look for a Consumer Product Safety Commission label stating that the crib meets Commission Standards. Resist hand-me-down or second-hand mattresses that may not exactly fit the crib. Make sure crib is painted with lead-free paint. Cribs manufactured prior to 1974, when lead paint became illegal for cribs, may have been repainted with paint containing lead.

■ The mattress should fit tightly, with no room for the baby to squeeze between it and the sides. If you can fit more than two fingers between the mattress and the crib, the mattress is too small. The firmer the mattress, the safer. Make sure the mattress support is securely attached to the headboard and footboard. Check the support system. To do this, push the mattress from the top, then the bottom. If the hanger support dislodges, it needs to be fixed or replaced. The four metal hangers supporting the mattress and support board must be secured in their notches by safety clips.

■ The slats should be spaced no more than 2-3/8" apart so that the baby's head can't get caught. The slats should be sturdy, firmly attached and there should be no crossbars on the sides. Hardware should be safe and secure. Check hardware for sharp points or edges, holes or cracks where your baby's fingers can get pinched or stuck. Check to be sure no screws or bolts are missing and that all secure and tight.

■ Bumper pads must fit around the entire crib, tie or snap into place and have at least six ties. Trim off excess length to prevent baby from becoming entangled in them or chewing them.

■ Check the drop sides. To prevent baby from releasing the drop sides, each one should be secured with two locking devices. Check to be certain that the drop side latches securely hold the sides in a raised position. When the sides are lowered, they should be at least four inches above the mattress.

■ Avoid cribs with fancy posts that have large crevices. Infants have strangled between the posts and crib. Avoid cribs with decorative knobs and cutouts. Baby's clothing can get caught on these. This may lead to strangulation.

■ Rub your hands over the wood surfaces. Check for cracks and splinters. If the baby is a chewer, cover the guardrails with nontoxic plastic chewer guards.

■ Place the crib in a safe area in the room: not against a window, nor near cords from blinds or draperies.

■ Check crib toys, mobiles, pacifiers and clothing to make sure there are no strings longer than eight inches.

I'm a Safe and Happy Baby

Stroller

* Choose a stroller that has a wide wheel base and rear wheels well behind the weight of the baby. When the baby leans over to the side or rocks backward the stroller will not tip. If the stroller has a reclining seat, check to be certain it can't tip backward when the baby lies down.

* If the stroller has a shopping basket, it must be located low on the back and directly over or in front of the rear wheels.

* Test the brakes. They should be easy to use. Brakes on two wheels are better than one. The brakes must be out of your child's reach so that they cannot be disengaged. Don't forget to use the brakes!

* Check all nuts and bolts for sharp edges and to be certain they are tight.

* Be sure that latching devices fasten securely. Strollers with two latching devices are safer than one. The latching device should prevent the stroller or canopy from folding or collapsing accidentally.

* When collapsing or opening the stroller, be careful of fingers . . . yours and baby's. There should be no exposed coil springs or any other moving parts that can pinch.

* The stroller should have "easy to use" seat belts that are securely attached to the frame.

High Chair

*   Some people use a portable chair (that attaches to the kitchen table) in place of a high chair. Be sure the seat is secure before placing the baby in the chair and the seat is strong enough to support the weight of the child.

*   Choose a chair that has a wide base. This provides good balance and stability.

*   Periodically check for splinters, loose screws and a wobbly base.

*   Check to see that the high chair tray is latched on both sides. When seated, baby may push against the tray.

*   Lock the tray. Test to be certain that it stays in position.

*   Do not depend on the tray to restrain the baby. Be sure the safety belt is attached to the chair. The belt should be easy to fasten and unfasten and should be independent of the tray.

*   Place the chair away from hazards such as stoves, windows, shelves and hanging drapery cords.

*   If the highchair is a folding one, it must have a secure locking device.

*   Be aware of holes or openings that could catch buttons, fingers or toes.

Changing Table

*   Choose a table with safety straps to hold the child in place and to prevent falls.

*   Choose a model which has safety latches on doors and drawers.

*   The shelves should be enclosed with doors. This will prevent your child from getting to the supplies.

*   Check that the drawers have safety stops on them so that they cannot be pulled out all the way.

*   Never leave a baby alone on a changing table, even for a brief moment. Place your hand on the child gently when you turn away to reach for clothing or for any other reason.

> When your child is out playing,
> you should be there as well.

Walker

The American Academy of Pediatrics does not recommend walkers any more. Walkers do not facilitate motor or muscle development and are one of the biggest causes of injuries in babies. Should you decide to use a walker, keep these things in mind:

*   Choose a walker with wheels that are sturdy and ride smoothly.

*   Choose a walker with a wheel base that is wider and longer than the seating area. This will reduce the chance of tipping. A walker should be stable so that it does not tip over if the child leans to one side or attempts to pick up something.

*   If there are coil springs, they should be covered with plastic for protection. Check all metal and plastic parts to be certain there are no sharp edges. Check locking devices. They should be strong and secure; then the walker will not collapse when in use.

Safety Harness

A safety harness with horse reins is helpful when you take an active toddler for a walk. With a harness, your child will have room to explore, but you can bring him or her toward you when it is necessary (crossing a street, coming upon broken glass, neighborhood dog, or other unsafe condition.) Using the reins is easier than trying to keep hold of a hand.

*   Use a safety harness to keep your child in a safe situation. He or she can often dash away even if you are there. A harness prevents this from occurring.

*   Do not use a harness to confine your child for long periods of time.

*   Provide constant supervision.

*   Do not attach the child to a tree, fence or other piece of equipment with the harness reins.

<u>Carriers</u>

You may find that a carrier is handy for carrying a new baby. The baby is close enough to you and both your hands are free for doing other things. Never use a backpack carrier before your baby is four or five months old and the neck is strong enough to withstand jolts.

* The carrier should be well made.

* Select a carrier that fits your child.

* The leg openings should be small enough to prevent the baby from slipping and big enough to avoid leg chafing.

* Try the carrier before buying.

* Never lean over when wearing a carrier. Lower yourself by bending at the knees.

* Check the carrier for torn seams or loose straps before you put it on.

* Choose a carrier that has a head support.

Front Pack /Sling Carrier

* Some carrier models are designed so that your baby can nurse while being carried.

* Choose a carrier that has safety straps with strong stitching.

* Use safety straps at all times.

* Carrier should be washable.

Backpack

*   Some parents find a backpack useful. Others skip this and prefer to use a stroller.

*   Try a backpack on with your child before buying it.

*   The carrier should be comfortable for your back and roomy enough for the child.

*   Check the straps. They should be wide and padded so that they don't dig into your shoulders. A good backpack will have a hip support strap to distribute your baby's weight more evenly.

*   The frame should be strong, sturdy, and lightweight.

*   Use safety restraining straps at all times.

*   You should be able to manage loading and unloading the child by yourself. If this is difficult, obtain assistance every time you use the backpack.

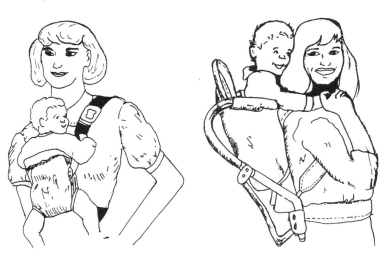

Front Pack/Sling Carrier   Backpack

Infant Seat

An infant seat allows you to seat your baby safely. Place baby in the seat for short periods of time.

> Never leave a baby unattended
> in an infant seat on a counter top,
> even for a second.

Use the safety belt in the infant seat and place the seat with the baby on a carpeted floor.

There are two types of infant seats:

1. The first type is a cloth bouncing seat that fits on a metal frame. The seat is comfortable for baby and bounces with the baby's motion. It provides support for a new baby and is stable for an older baby.

2. The second type is a bulky plastic seat. It is durable and has a carrying handle. Some models have a storage compartment and may rock as well. This type of seat may be awkward to carry and may not be as portable as some mothers would like.

Never use an infant seat to secure a baby in the car. A specially designed and approved car seat must be used for infants and children. (Law in most states.)

Infant Seat

A New
Beginning

Toys

Playtime is a natural activity for every child at any age. Infants enjoy the simple things around them. Play provides opportunities for your child to learn and grow mentally, socially and physically.

Toy selection should consider the following points:
* well constructed, safe and durable
* interesting and appealing to the child
* suited to the child's physical capabilities
* suited to the child's mental and social development

The recall of an unsafe toy may remove it from the marketplace. This often occurs after a child has been injured or killed. The U.S. Consumer Product Safety Commission suggests the following guidelines:

■ Don't let your child play with pointed objects such as knives, scissors, knitting needles, etc. Some toys may be dismantled and may reveal sharp objects.

■ Be alert for items which could be swallowed. Tiny toys should be avoided.

■ Toys intended for older children should not be given to a younger child. A toy which is safe for a three-year-old could be dangerous for a two year old.

■ Any toy which requires plugging into an electrical socket is not safe for younger children. Try battery operated toys first, but check to be sure they are designed for toddler use. Wind up toys are even better.

■ Keep things with strings away from babies. A toddler should NEVER take a pull toy to bed.

■ Toys such as cap pistols or guns which make loud noises can damage a child's hearing.

■ Toys which shoot things, such as darts, rockets and arrows, are unsafe for young children. Be careful of rubber tips . . . they may be removed to leave a sharp end. A rubber tip can also cause injury.

TOY SELECTION
OTHER ITEMS TO CONSIDER

* A toy should be too big to fit into a child's mouth.

* Be careful of plastic toys that are brittle, thin and might break easily leaving sharp and jagged edges. Bend the toy (before buying it) to see how breakable the plastic is.

* Stuffed toys should be made well. The stuffing should stay intact and not end up inside the child. Stay away from toys with decorative features that might come off. The eyes from dolls and stuffed animals need to be checked prior to buying. The stuffing should be non-toxic. There should be no sharp pieces in the toy, just in case it rips open.

* Any paint should be non-toxic.

* Make sure unsafe toys are out of reach. Balloons, balls, beads, Legos®, and other small objects (less than 1-1/2") can lead to trouble by ending up in a baby's airway.

* Do not allow a child under six years old to blow up a balloon. You blow it up instead. Keep balloons safely out of reach when not in use. Pick up and safely dispose of all broken pieces.

* Avoid letting babies play with uninflated balloons; these can cause choking. If a balloon pops, gather up the pieces quickly and keep them away from the baby. Always supervise a child playing with an inflated balloon.

* Throw away plastic wrappings immediately. Children love to play with wrapping paper as well as plastic garment bags. These are dangerous...may lead to suffocation.

* Before buying or giving a child a toy, make sure there are no small parts which could cause choking: beads, doll shoes, buttons, squeaker buttons in squeak toys, stuffing made of pellets.

* Avoid toy chests with attached lids that can fall on a child and cause injury and strangulation. Hinged lids should stay open by themselves, without propping.

* Do not give your child a toy intended for an older child thinking that it will be a good challenge and the child will "grow into it."

* A toy should be suited to your child's age and ability level. Look for age recommendations on toys. Check the toy carefully before allowing your child to play with it. Toys used by older siblings should be put away.

* Look for safety label: Underwriter Laboratories ("UL approved") on electrical items, "flame resistant/flame retardant" on fabrics and "washable/hygienic materials" on stuffed toys.

* Repair or throw away broken toys.

* Never allow toys to be left on or near stairways.

* It is important to protect your child from unsafe toys as well as unsafe use of toys. When old enough, the child should be taught to use toys properly and safely. By carefully selecting toys and supervising your child at play you will have chosen the best way to protect your child from toy-related injuries.

Part Four

SAFETY OUTSIDE THE HOME

YARD SAFETY

Through the eyes of a child, the yard looks very big; there is a lot of territory to explore. Everything looks interesting and fascinating. The great outdoors, however, does have some "booby" traps. Look at the entire play area from your child's point of view. Ask yourself: "What is out there that can hurt my child?" Then, make a safety walk of the entire area. Remove the hazards as you go ... to make play time as safe as possible.

General Safety Guidelines

* Fence in the yard area. If this is not possible, restrict the child from playing in an area where there is street or driveway access.
* Check to see that your yard is "climb proof." Do you have toys which are safe to climb, such as rubber tires? All other climbing devices should be removed.
* Supervise all play. Do NOT leave your child alone. Stay close by and watch your child's play activities.

Lawn Care

Do not use lawn equipment while children are playing in the yard.

Ride-on mowers can be dangerous; a child riding on a mower with a parent can easily lead to an accident. The child can fall off and be run over.

Use lawn chemicals sparingly, if at all. Check all products out with your poison control center. NEVER leave containers open. Dispose of containers and any unused products based on recommendations on the product label or from your local authorities.

Sandboxes

A sandbox can provide hours of creative fun but sand also invites animals to use it as litter. For that reason, a sandbox, when not in use, should be covered. A cover will also keep the sand dry. Use a window screen as a sand "sifter." This will remove sharp objects and other pieces of material. Buy sand that has been made and sold intended for play. Replace at least once a year.

Decks

Most deck injuries among toddlers are caused by falls. Stair guards are vital, both at the top of the stairs as well as at the bottom of the stairs. Line the openings in the railings with mesh. Often a child can get stuck in them if the rail openings are wide. Keep furniture away from railings so that your child cannot climb over the rails by standing on the furniture.

Hazards

- Railings or fences should be narrow enough so that your child's head cannot be trapped.

- Put away lawn equipment such as rakes and other tools.

- Make sure that driveways, walkways and patios have smooth surfaces.

- Clotheslines should be out of a child's reach.

- Place deck furniture away from all railings.

- Floor-to-ceiling glass doors should have decals on them.

- Store propane grills so that a child cannot reach the knobs.

- Check lawn furniture for exposed screws or nails.

- Lock garbage pails in an enclosed area.

- Remove broken glass, twigs, sharp metal and loose stones. Fill holes or deep indentations in the ground to prevent tripping.

- Check outdoor electrical outlets. Put safety covers over all outlets.

- Check wood surfaces for peeling paint, loose boards and exposed screws or nails.

- Store garden hose. Do not leave hose exposed to the hot sun. The water may become hot enough to scald a child.

- Check area for nests which may be home for bees, wasps, hornets or termites.

©

Playground Equipment

Play equipment such as swing sets and slides have provided hours of fun to children. In choosing, setting up the equipment and during daily usage, keep these safety rules in mind:

- The vertical and horizontal spaces on playground equipment, such as between the rungs of a ladder, should be less than 3 1/2" wide or more than 9" wide, so that your child's head will not get caught.

- Equipment should be anchored securely.

- Swing sets should be made of material which is soft, such as, rubber, plastic, or canvas.

- The seats should be U shaped. The seat should have a strap around the back to keep the child from falling backward.

- Some sets have a safety seat which has a safety bar and crotch strap.

- All playground equipment should be installed over soft material, such as sand, shredded mulch, shredded tires, or sawdust. Should a child fall, this will absorb the force of the fall.

- The equipment should be least 6 feet away from a fence or other type of obstruction.

- There should be no sharp edges, protruding nuts or bolts, or splintering surfaces exposed.

©

Garden Plants and Trees

Plants and trees which add beauty to your yard may be harmful to your child. Check your yard for harmful plants. Replace if possible or keep your child away from these plants with fences, etc. If you are unsure of the type of plant in the yard, check with your local nursery or farm bureau service. Never keep harmful plants or cut flowers that are harmful in your house.

Non-harmful Garden Plants and Trees

Asparagus fern	Gardenia	Norfolk pine
Bamboo	Geranium	Pansy
Bougainvillea	Hens and chickens	Petunia
Camellia	Hibiscus	Piggyback plant
Coleus	Honeysuckle	Rose
Crab apple	Jade plant	Rubber plant
Dahlia	Laurel	Schefflera
Dandelion	Maidenhair fern	Snapdragon
Eucalyptus	Marigold	Tulip
Forsythia	Mint	Yucca

Most of these plants are grown outside. They often find themselves in the house as cut flowers or a decorative piece; i.e., Azaleas, Irises, Roses.

Harmful Garden Plants and Trees

Amaryllis	Hydrangea	Poppy
Azalea	Iris	Rhubarb leaves
Bird of paradise	Lilac	Sweet pea
Daffodil	Lily of the valley	Tomato plant
Daphne	Mistletoe	stems & leaves
Delphinium (larkspur)	Morning glory	Wisteria
English Ivy	Oleander*	
Foxglove	Poison Ivy	**Trees****
Holly berries	Poison Oak	Peach
Hyacinth	Poison sumac	Plum
		Cherry
		Apricot
		Nectarine

*poisonous - eliminate from yard
**Leaves, stems, bark and seed pits are harmful

"I wonder if this is good to eat?"

IF YOUR BABY EATS A PLANT
FOLLOW THESE STEPS

CHECK BABY Check baby's hand and mouth for any pieces of the plant that may be remaining. Check the hands, eyes, and lips for redness or blistering. Check the tongue and inside of the mouth for cuts, redness, swelling and blistering.

CHECK PLANT What list is it on? Harmless or dangerous list? Examine the plant. Look at the plants that the child can reach easily first. Look for spilled dirt, broken leaves, broken vase or container, or any other signs that the child has handled the plant.

CALL POISON CONTROL If the plant is suspicious or you do not know whether it is harmful or not, call your local Poison Control Center. If there is a tag on the plant, give the full name. If no tag is available, describe the plant.

TAKE YOUR CHILD TO THE EMERGENCY ROOM

If you are still uncertain and suspicious, take your child and the plant (or large portion, if plant is very big), to

the emergency room. While you are with the child, a family member can take the plant cutting to a nursery for identification. This information can be phoned to the emergency room while you are enroute or already there.

Pool Safety

Infant and toddler swimming lessons are very popular. Many children seem to enjoy these programs. Swimming is a pleasurable sport or pastime and at some point should be part of your child's experience. There are some "cautions" to consider.

Infant programs that encourage submersion of the head for more than a few seconds should be avoided. Swallowed pool water can be dangerous. An excessive intake of water can lower the baby's sodium level and cause seizures.

If an infant is not being held, and goes under, he or she can inhale enough water in the first 10 seconds to cause drowning. Go slowly with lessons. If pushed or hurried, a child can develop a fear of water.

If you want your infant or toddler acquainted with water, try a wading pool first. Concentrate on having "fun" first, not learning how to swim. If the child enjoys the water, swimming will be learned quickly.

Even if your baby or toddler does learn to swim, this does not eliminate the need for you to supervise all water activities. Do not allow the ability of the child to "dog-paddle" to give you a false sense of security. Never leave a child alone near the pool...even for a second!

Water Safety Tips

* If you have a backyard pool, be sure you have a clear view of the water at all times.

* A pool must be secured by a locked gate. Above ground and in-ground pools must be fenced on all sides.

* If you use a pool cover, do not consider this as a substitute for supervision. Never allow your child to climb on the pool cover while it is on the pool.

* Keep toys away from the pool area. A young child playing with the toys can accidentally fall into the water.

* Move lawn furniture to an area outside the fence where it cannot be used for fence climbing.

* Use only battery-operated radios near the pool. Remove all electrical yard and garden tools.

* Remove the entrance ladder from an above ground pool when no one is swimming.

* Never let a young child in a walker near a pool.

Swimming Rules
Good Pool-side Manners

* No running on the pool deck.
* No dunking.
* No swimming alone.
* No tickling in the pool.
* No diving into inner tubes or jumping on other inflatable toys.
* No glass in the pool area.
* No splashing or making big waves near a small infant.

Pool Drains

Swimming pool drains can cause dangerous accidents. Some states have put in rules regarding the design and construction of pools, including those relating to drain safety. New or rebuilt pools may be required to have skimmers (water level drains built into the sides) and two bottom drains, instead of just one. This will reduce the suction force. Without a grate covering a pool drain, the suction is enough to pull part of the intestine out of the rectum if the child sits on the drain. This can result in a life threatening situation.

There is a need to check safety equipment each day in community pools and private pools. Follow the water safety tips outlined in this section. Swimming should and can be fun.

While precautions need to be taken to prevent accidents in the backyard,  your child should think that yard play and swimming are "fun time." Children need to explore and may get bumps and bruises. Excessive protection prevents them from discovering the world outside. The key is to teach children appropriate behavior, such as, not to eat dirt, sand, or grass. Your supervision and child's knowledge will lead to a "safe and fun" yard experience.

Car Safety

Every time your baby rides in a car, even during the first ride from the hospital, he or she should be in a car seat. It should be a car seat, not an infant carrier or infant seat. Buy a car seat before the baby is born and use it every time the baby rides in the car.

Car crashes are the biggest danger to your child's life and health. Most automobile injuries and deaths can be prevented by the use of car safety seats. Not only crashes, but swerves and sudden stops can cause serious injuries to children who are not correctly restrained in a car seat.

All states have child passenger protection laws that require small children usually up to four years of age, to ride in certified child car seats whether they are in the front or back seat.

Safety Seats For Children

Infant Car Seats   Infant car seats are designed to be used from birth to 9-12 months, or to a weight of about 20 pounds. Place the seat preferably in the center of the back seat. The car seat must face the rear of the car so that the baby's stronger back and shoulders can absorb the force of a crash, swerve, or sudden stop.

The safest place for children of any age is in the back seat of the car. Whether the infant is in the front or the back seat, the infant must face the rear. All straps should be snug. *HOUSEHOLD INFANT CARRIERS AND CLOTH CARRIERS ARE NOT DESIGNED TO PROTECT AN INFANT IN A CAR AND SHOULD NOT BE USED.*

Convertible Seat

A convertible seat is a combination of an infant seat and toddler seat. It can be used from birth to about four years old or a weight of 40 pounds. The seat should face backwards until the child is 9-12 months old or weighs approximately 20 pounds. The seat can then be converted to a forward facing seat. Fasten the car seat with the vehicle seat belt through the car seat frame, according to the manufacturer's instructions.

Booster Seat

When your child has outgrown the convertible seat or weighs about 40 pounds, a belt positioning booster seat can be used. This seat is practical for the child who has outgrown the convertible seat and is too small to use the car's safety belt. Some booster seats are reversible and provide a medium height for smaller children and lower height for taller children. This allows for the adjustment of the shoulder harness.

Harnessed Booster Seat

Baby's Safety and Comfort

Dress baby in clothing with legs while in the car seat. Do not use a bunting that prevents you from securing the car seat straps snugly between your baby's legs.

Do not wrap the baby in a blanket before placing him or her in the car seat. It will be difficult to keep the harness straps snug and high on the baby's shoulders.

Adjust the harness to accommodate clothing...lightweight in summer or thicker and heavier in the winter.

Use a car seat according to manufacturer's instructions and your vehicle owner's manual and use it every time your child rides in a motor vehicle.

It is unsafe to use a seat that is too large or too small for your child. Make certain that the seat is the correct style for your child's age, size and development.

Some cars have seat belts with buckles that slide freely on the belts. This type of belt loosens easily and cannot secure a car seat safely. A locking clip will be needed to keep the buckle from sliding. If your car has this type of seat belt, select a car seat with locking clips.

Locking Clip

Purchasing Tips

Select only child car seats that meet U.S. Department of Transportation requirements. Look for this label-"This child restraint system conforms to all applicable federal motor vehicle safety standards"-with the date of manufacture after January 1, 1981.

Pets in the Home

Choosing a Pet

It is best not to introduce a new pet into the household during your child's first two years. Should you decide to do so, keep this in mind:

Certain pets and babies do not mix. Cats and kittens usually accept babies. There are breeds of dogs which are "baby friendly." Avoid breeds of dogs that are unpredictable and have high strung personalities. A Veterinarian or pet store staff can provide advice regarding a gentle breed.

What To Do After the Baby Is Born (Baby and Dog)

Before you bring the baby home, bring home articles that have touched the baby, i.e. blankets, layette.

Let the dog become familiar with the scent before you wash the blankets. Slowly introduce the dog to toys and blankets that have the baby's smell on them.

At Coming Home Time

Before the baby is brought into the house, the mother should go in and greet the dog by herself. Give the pet a genuine "hello." Assure him that you are O.K. Bring the baby into the house. Let the dog sniff the baby's articles again as you hold them. Observe the responses. If he continues to be happy, wags his tail and shows no signs of aggressive behavior, continue on in your "get acquainted" time. The person whom the

dog obeys readily should hold the dog on a leash commanding the dog to sit...while praising him. At this time the pet should be able to see but not touch the baby. Do this several times a day, gradually bringing the dog closer each time. Watch the dog each time to observe his responses. If the dog behaves and is under verbal control after several introductions, you can take him off the leash. Let him wander in the room while the baby is being held. You can pet the dog while you are cradling the baby. Don't forget the praise!

Take time daily to have fun with the dog without the baby being present. Throwing his favorite toy is a good playtime choice. Do not play tug of war, wrestle or chase. These games tell the dog that he is in charge. You must always be the leader.

You can all be "One Big Happy Family."

Safety Around a Pet

A two-year old can understand how to behave safely around a pet. Teach your child not to grab the dog's dish or bone. Put the pet's feeding dish out of the reach of a toddler.

* Teach your child how to approach a strange dog. Have the child stand still while the animal sniffs and circles. Speak to the dog in a soothing calm voice.

* Provide supervision. A reliable family pet will probably not turn on a toddler, however, it is best to prevent a situation where this could occur.

* Never give a toddler the responsibility of taking care of a pet.

* Flea collars are toxic and should be handled carefully. Your child should not be allowed to chew on a collar.

* There are lessons which need to be taught. Hold your pet; show the child how to stroke the animal. Speak quietly while this is happening; compliment the pet for good behavior.

If your dog guards objects such as food, balls, bones or toys, he must learn that this is unacceptable behavior. You may be able to tell the difference between dog toys and baby toys, but your baby can't. If your baby accidentally picks up a dog toy, your dog could feel threatened and bite him or her. You, as the primary caretaker, must be able to take any item out of your dog's mouth.

It your dog jumps on people, it's very important to train him to keep all four feet on the floor. The dog can do serious harm by jumping on you while you're holding your baby. To prevent this from happening, teach your dog to sit and stay rather than jump. When he obeys, use lots of praise to make sitting and staying a wonderful thing. Once your dog has mastered these commands, begin to add distractions; coo over dolls dressed in the baby's layette; wheel around the baby carriage; get tapes of babies crying.

Introduce the dog to the new sounds and smells of a baby. Whatever you do, use lots of praise and love.

Babies treat animals like toys. They may pull ears and tails and put fingers in an animal's mouth or eyes. Provide for a "get acquainted" time when they first meet.

Never leave the baby and pet alone. "Snappy" dogs can be unpredictable. A cat may jump into a bassinet and try to snuggle. Dogs are often unaware of their own strength and can cause injury out of excitement and happiness.

Young children explore by touching. Be prepared to protect the animal or child, or both as needed.

It's Worth the Effort

Be Observant

Accidents tend to happen more often when you are:
*   Running late for an appointment.
*   Moving into a new home.
*   Caring for an ill sibling.
*   The only caregiver at home (your spouse is away for an extended time period).
*   Changing babysitters or day care centers.
*   Going through marital stress or divorce.
*   Bringing home the new baby.
*   Vacationing.

These home hazards can cause an accident:
*   Steps in need of repair
*   Poor lighting
*   Cluttered floors
*   Frayed electrical cords
*   Sharp objects
*   Chemicals
*   Poisons

**Change what you can change.
Protect yourself from what you cannot change.**

Part Five

CHOOSING A BABYSITTER

Choosing a Babysitter

Every couple differs in their ideas about going out together after the birth of their baby. One couple might decide that they will not go anywhere without taking their infant with them. Another couple might feel the need to have a few hours alone with each other within a few weeks of adding the new child to their household. Newborns are portable; you may decide you don't need a babysitter at first. Eventually, everyone finds some occasion when the baby needs to be with a caretaker for a few hours.

You will want to give careful thought to the selection of the person who will care for your baby. If your family lives nearby, you may feel most comfortable in leaving the infant with a family member. Many new grandparents are thrilled to babysit; others may feel uncomfortable around a new baby or infant. You may find a neighbor, friend, babysitting co-op or someone from the church or community center. Avoid choosing someone from a bulletin board ad, unless you insist upon a number of references and interview the candidate.

Guidelines

* Get recommendations from friends in the neighborhood.
* Interview someone you already know who is interested.
* Screen first, ask for references and résumé <u>before</u> you interview.
* After choosing a sitter, familiarize the person with the baby's routines.
* Leave a number where you may be reached.
* Give a time frame as to how long you will be gone.
* Be sure sitters know how to call the fire department, poison control center: the numbers you have listed near your phone (refer to page 77).
* Tell the babysitter to keep the door locked at all times.
* Review how you want him/her to respond if someone comes to the door.
* Review child safety measures (pages 4 and 5).
* Review baby's schedule: bath, feeding, playtime, bedtime, etc.
* Clarify what the sitter is allowed or not allowed to do: watch TV, smoke, telephone time, eat snacks, have visitors or personal friends.
* When you get home, ask how the time was spent, about any problems, broken rules or other issues.
* Always accompany the babysitter home, even if he or she lives across the street. This will not be necessary if the babysitter is a mature adult and is going to drive home.

Interviewing Candidates

Before you start to interview candidates, make a list of questions you will ask. Put the <u>most</u> important questions at the top. If the person does not answer the questions to your satisfaction, you may not need to complete the entire list and thus eliminate wasting time.

As you listen to the answers, get a feel for the person's nurturing/caring abilities as well as flexibility. Get a sense of whether you can work with and trust this person. Watch how the individual interacts with the baby during the interview. Does he/she look directly at you and act natural or forced? Consider your overall feeling for this person. Is he/she kind, patient, flexible and caring? It is important to have the right match. If with the first interview you don't succeed, keep trying. After you have made your choice, agree upon a trial period of a few weeks to see if you, the babysitter and baby are happy.

Home
Safe
Home

Questions to Ask During the Interview

* Obtain name, address, phone number, references, résumé.

* What will you do if my baby cries? What comforting techniques have you used that work best for you?

* What would you like to know about the baby?

* What do you feel that a baby of this age needs most?

* Why do you want to look after infants?

* How will you play with the baby?

* How do you feel about holding the baby a lot?

* How will you put my baby to sleep?

* Tell me about your previous babysitting experiences.

* What would you do if the baby begins to choke on a toy?

* How will you handle feeding the baby? (If you are breastfeeding, does he/she understand the importance of giving your pumped breastmilk?)

* What are the most common accidents you feel may happen? How would you respond to each one?

* Tell me about your last job. Why did you leave it? (Previous job should be listed on the résumé.)

* Do you have children of your own? What are their ages?

* How is your health? Are you a smoker? (Smokers and babies do not mix.) Do you drink? If so, how much and how often? Do you use other drugs? (Get a sense of comfort the person has in answering these questions. Is the individual agitated or at ease?)

Following these guidelines should allow you to have a relaxed time away from your baby. You will have a measure of peace of mind, knowing that your child is safe and is being cared for by a responsible sitter who has been screened and prepared by you.

Part Six

BE PREPARED

ACCIDENTS HAPPEN: BE PREPARED

Accidents can and do happen; prepare yourself, your family members, and your home.

Things to do:

* You and your household members should take a first aid and CPR Course. Renew your CPR card every year.
* Keep a well stocked First Aid Kit.
* Know how to call for help and who should be called.

First Aid Kit

You may purchase a First Aid Kit. Be sure the kit has a safety lock. Place it out of reach of toddlers. Check the kit, and add items from the following list to supplement the products already included in the kit. All medicines should have current dosage directions for infants and children. Update as the family grows.

HOME FIRST AID KIT

Acetaminophen pain reliever, liquid and suppositories (Tylenol)
Adhesive tape
Alcohol swabs
Antibiotic ointment
Antihistamine - (Benadryl) for insect stings
Antiseptic solution (Betadine, Hibiclens)
Bandage (triangular)
Band-aids (various sizes)
Calamine lotion
Cotton balls
Cotton tip applicators (Q-tips)
Elastic wrap (Ace bandage)
Small flashlight or pen light
Gauze - 2X2", 4X4", non-stick, and Kling-wrap

Hydrogen peroxide
Instant ice pack
Ipecac syrup
Mild soap
Measuring spoon or calibrated dropper
Nasal aspirator
Salt water nose drops (saline) or saline spray
Petroleum jelly
Safety pins
Scissors (blunt ends)
Steri-strips
Thermometer (rectal) glass or digital
Tongue depressors
Tweezers

©

CPR and First Aid Courses

CPR (cardiopulmonary resuscitation) teaches you how to restore breathing and resuscitate the heart. Your local American Heart Association, the American Red Cross, hospitals, and other health care agencies offer courses. There may be a nominal fee or the course may be free of charge.

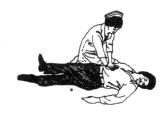

First Aid courses teach you how to react in an urgent or accident situation. You will be taught what to do until help arrives and what you can handle yourself.

Calling for help: Beside each telephone in your house, place emergency phone numbers and directions.

Emergency Phone List

Doctor or Pediatrician:_____

Hospital Emergency: _____

Paramedics: _____

Police and Fire: _____

Poison Control Center: _____

Parent Work Number: _____

Leave a phone number for babysitters where you or other suitable adults can be consulted in case there is a question or an emergency.

Make the list easy to read, phone numbers clear and readily available for family members, babysitters, and others.

There are small labels with paste on the back which can be placed on each phone. Insert information listed above on the labels.

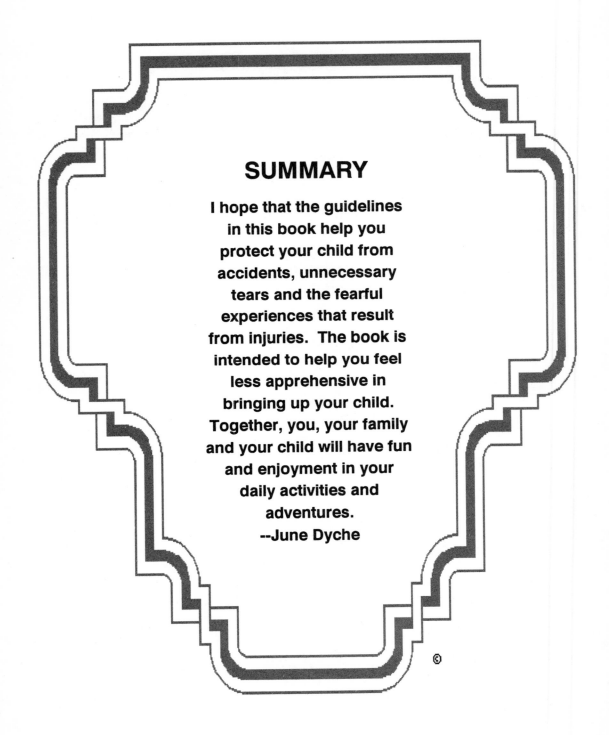

SUMMARY

I hope that the guidelines in this book help you protect your child from accidents, unnecessary tears and the fearful experiences that result from injuries. The book is intended to help you feel less apprehensive in bringing up your child. Together, you, your family and your child will have fun and enjoyment in your daily activities and adventures.

--June Dyche

INDEX

DISCOUNTS ARE AVAILABLE FOR QUANTITY ORDERS TO PHYSICIANS, CLINICS, AND OTHER ORGANIZATIONS.

ORDER FORM

FOR ADDITIONAL COPIES

Quantity and Price

Please send me _____ books at $7.95 each.
Postage & Handling: $1.05 per book.
TOTAL PRICE: $_____

Billing Address

Company Name
Your Name
Title
Address
City   State   Zip
Telephone (   )

Shipping Address (not a post office box)
(Complete only if different from address above)

Street
City   State   Zip

Payment Options

☐ 1. I have enclosed a check.

☐ 2. Please bill my: ☐ Master Card   ☐ VISA

Card #   Exp. Date
Cardholder's signature

PLEASE MAIL THIS FORM AND PAYMENT TO:
Tri-Oak Education
3698 Armstrong Valley Road • Murfreesboro, TN 37129
FAX (615) 849-8825

FOR ORDERS OF 10 OR MORE, FAX YOUR REQUEST FOR DISCOUNT INFORMATION.

DISCOUNTS ARE AVAILABLE FOR QUANTITY ORDERS TO PHYSICIANS, CLINICS, AND OTHER ORGANIZATIONS.

ORDER FORM

FOR ADDITIONAL COPIES

Quantity and Price

Please send me _____ books at $7.95 each.
Postage & Handling: $1.05 per book.
TOTAL PRICE: $_____

Billing Address

Company Name		
Your Name		
Title		
Address		
City	State	Zip
Telephone ( )		

Shipping Address (not a post office box)
(Complete only if different from address above)

Street		
City	State	Zip

Payment Options

☐ 1. I have enclosed a check.

☐ 2. Please bill my: ☐ Master Card   ☐ VISA

Card #	Exp. Date
Cardholder's signature	

PLEASE MAIL THIS FORM AND PAYMENT TO:
Tri-Oak Education
3698 Armstrong Valley Road • Murfreesboro, TN 37129
FAX (615) 849-8825

FOR ORDERS OF 10 OR MORE, FAX YOUR REQUEST FOR DISCOUNT INFORMATION.

DISCOUNTS ARE AVAILABLE FOR QUANTITY ORDERS TO PHYSICIANS, CLINICS, AND OTHER ORGANIZATIONS.

ORDER FORM

FOR ADDITIONAL COPIES

Quantity and Price

Please send me _____ books at $7.95 each.

Postage & Handling: $1.05 per book.

TOTAL PRICE: $_____

Billing Address

Company Name

Your Name

Title

Address

City   State   Zip

Telephone (   )

Shipping Address (not a post office box)
(Complete only if different from address above)

Street

City   State   Zip

Payment Options

☐ 1. I have enclosed a check.

☐ 2. Please bill my: ☐ Master Card   ☐ VISA

Card #   Exp. Date

Cardholder's signature

PLEASE MAIL THIS FORM AND PAYMENT TO:
Tri-Oak Education
3698 Armstrong Valley Road • Murfreesboro, TN 37129
FAX (615) 849-8825

FOR ORDERS OF 10 OR MORE, FAX YOUR REQUEST FOR DISCOUNT INFORMATION.